How to use these notes

Guided Rea~~ding~~

Walkthrough (pages 2–3)

A *walkthrough*, or book int~~roduction~~ ... group of children. During the walkth~~rough~~ ... ~~id~~eas and significant vocabulary they ...

Go through the whole of the ~~book~~ ... before the children start reading independently. The walkthrough notes on pages 2 and 3 of this booklet provide prompts for you to use, specific to *The Greedy King*. The questions, comments and suggestions alert children to ideas and vocabulary they will need in order to read independently and with full understanding.

Independent Reading (pages 4–5)

After doing a walkthrough, ask the children to read the text aloud, on their own, at their own pace. Observe the strategies each child uses, praising successful problem solving and expressive reading. Prompts are suggested for good phrasing, use of word-solving skills, predicting and checking the meaning, and actively monitoring the implications of the text, on pages 4 and 5.

After Independent Reading/ Returning to the text (page 6)

After the children have read the book independently, return to the text as a group to reinforce teaching points and to check children's understanding. On page 6, there are quick follow-up ideas for related text, sentence and word level work.

Responding to the text (pages 6–8)

It is important to encourage children to give a personal response to the text. Discussion ideas related to the book are on page 6.

These Teaching Notes also contain group activity ideas on page 7, and a Photocopy Master on page 8, for use after the guided reading session or in a follow-up literacy session.

Guided Reading Notes

Walkthrough

The Greedy King has been written in the style of a traditional story, so encourage the children to make comparisons with other traditional stories that they have read. Praise the children when they pick up similarities in the style of language, characters and the moral of the story.

Cover

Read the title and the back cover blurb to the children.

PROMPTS Who can guess what type of story this is going to be? (Prompt for *like a traditional* (or *old*) *story*.) Lots of traditional stories start with words like 'Once there was', don't they?

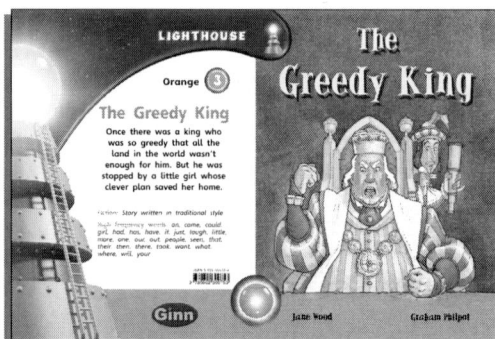

Pages 2–3

PROMPTS Ask the children to read the opening sentence of the story. What is the greedy king doing in the illustrations? What is happening as the story opens? The king looks angry – and can you see the capital letters and the exclamation mark which tell us that he's angry?

Walk through pages 4 and 5, discussing the illustrations with the children. Talk about the setting. How do we know the story is set a long time ago?

Pages 6–7

PROMPTS Look at the illustrations. What might the little girl be saying to the king? She has something to give to him. Ask the children to find the word *something*. It's something that no one else has ever seen before. Do you think the king will be tempted by her offer?

A little girl came to see the king. "Please sir," she said. "I have an idea. I can give you something much better than this land.

"I can give you something that no one else has ever seen before. If I give it to you, will you let us keep our land?"

Pages 10–11

PROMPTS What is the little girl carrying? Can you point to the word *basket*? Can you guess what's in her basket? Reinforce the fact that it is something that has never been seen before.

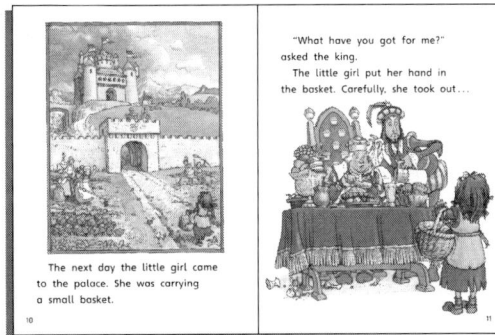

The next day the little girl came to the palace. She was carrying a small basket.

"What have you got for me?" asked the king.
The little girl put her hand in the basket. Carefully, she took out...

Stop the walkthrough at page 11, so that the children can discover what the little girl has during their own reading. Go back to the start of the book and ask the children to read independently.

Independent Reading

Observe each child as she or he is reading, and check for independent problem solving of unfamiliar words. Encourage the children to read with pace and expression appropriate to the grammar and punctuation, and to the growing anticipation in the plot.

Different children will find different challenges in the text. The examples below show where there are opportunities to prompt for specific strategies.

Pages 2–3

Next to the king's land there was <u>another</u> country where many people lived. The king wanted their land for himself.

There was once a very greedy king. He owned all the land that he could see, but he wanted more.

"I want more land!" he shouted. "More, more, MORE!"

2
3

another
"Look for known words within the word."

CHECK that the child reads with expression, taking account of the exclamation marks, capitalization and speech verb *shouted*.

Pages 4–5

He took his men to tell the people to leave their land.

"The king wants your land," said the men. "You have to get out – NOW!"

"Where can we go? What can we do? How can we live without our land?" the people asked.

The greedy king didn't care what happened to the people. He just wanted their land.

4
5

CHECK that the child reads with expression, taking account of the question marks.

Ask the child to read on, checking that he or she reads the repeated phrase *something that no one else has ever seen before* accurately, as the word order changes slightly.

Pages 8–9

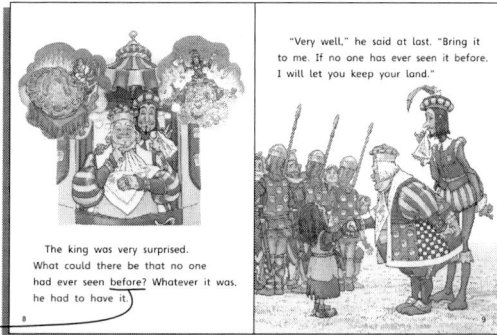

The king was very surprised. What could there be that no one had ever seen before? Whatever it was, he had to have it.

"Very well," he said at last. "Bring it to me. If no one has ever seen it before, I will let you keep your land."

whatever   before
"Look for known words within the word."

CHECK that the child can blend the phonemes *ur* and *i-e* in *surprised*, and check for meaning.

"Does the king think the girl can bring him something?"

Ask the child to read on, checking that she or he has picked up on the time connective *the next day*, and paused at the end of page 11 for the ellipsis.

Pages 12–13

... an egg. An ordinary, smooth, brown egg.

"An egg?" screamed the king. "Everyone in the world has seen an egg! You lose! I keep the land!"

ordinary
"Split the word into syllables. Think what would make sense."

CHECK that the child knows what the ellipsis is for.

"It tells us that the author wanted us to pause before finishing the sentence."

Page 16

CHECK that the child takes account of the comma.

"That comma tells us to pause for a moment. It adds to the effect of the sentence."

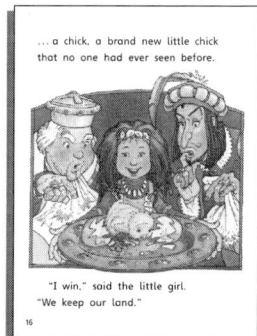

... a chick, a brand new little chick that no one had ever seen before.

"I win," said the little girl. "We keep our land."

5

Word knowledge – read unfamiliar words by identifying known words within words

Draw the children's attention to the words *something* and *before* on page 7. Ask them to work out what the words say by finding known words within the word. Ask them to find other examples of words within words in the text, for example, in *another*, *whatever*, *carefully*.

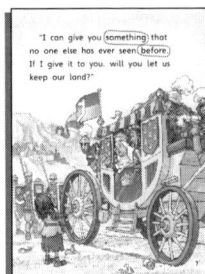

"I can give you something that no one else has ever seen before. If I give it to you, will you let us keep our land?"

Sentence knowledge – read with expression

Ask the children to reread page 5, this time concentrating on expression. Demonstrate the way our voices rise at the end of a question. How would the people have felt? Ask them to read page 13 again, paying attention to the verb *screamed* and the exclamation marks.

"Where can we go? What can we do? How can we live without our land?" the people asked.
The greedy king didn't care what happened to the people. He just wanted their land.

Text knowledge – discuss and compare story themes

Can the children think of any other traditional stories in which greedy or selfish people are taught a lesson? Examples known to the children might include *The Old Woman Who Lived in a Vinegar Bottle*, *The Selfish Giant*, *The Three Wishes*.

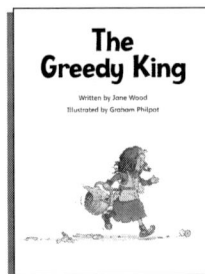

The Greedy King

Written by Jane Wood
Illustrated by Graham Philpot

Responding to the text

● Did anyone in the group guess what the little girl was taking to the King? Could it have been anything else?

● What sort of character is the King? Ask the children to give evidence from the text to support their views.

● What is the main theme of the story? Could it happen in real life?

Group activity ideas

① Tell the story

AIM to retell the story of *The Greedy King* in sequence (*NLS: Y2 T1 T3, 4*)

YOU WILL NEED
- tape recorder
- flip chart
- copies of *The Greedy King*

WHAT TO DO Ask the children to take it in turns to tell an episode from the story. Note down the episodes as they are told, on the flip chart. Refer to the text and talk about the sequence of events as written. If necessary, discuss and make alterations to the sequence of events noted on the flip chart. Next ask the group to retell the story using the notes on the flip chart for reference. They may take turns to recount different episodes. Record their version of the story. Listen to the tape and discuss differences between their told version and the text.

② Punctuation

AIM to recognize the effect commas and exclamation marks have on reading aloud (*NLS: Y2 T1 S3*)

YOU WILL NEED
- flip chart or overhead transparency

WHAT TO DO Reproduce the text from page 2 without full stops, commas and exclamation marks, e.g.

There was once a very greedy king he owned all the land that he could see but he wanted more
"I want more land" he shouted
"More more MORE"

Tell the children to rewrite the text with full stops, commas and exclamation marks. They should then practise reading the text aloud with expression appropriate to the punctuation marks.

7

Spot the 'ow' sound

The men shouted, "You have
to get out NOW!"

"How can we live without

our land?" the people asked.

ou	ow

Ask the children to underline the words which contain the *ow* phoneme. Encourage them to look for different spellings. The children can then list the words in the table provided, and add some more of their own.

The Greedy King   *(NLS: Y2 T1 W3)*